EXPRESS YOURSELF!

Activities and Adventures in EXPRESSIONISM

by Sammy, 8

JOYCE RAIMONDO

Watson-Guptill Publications/New York

For my lifelong friend, Lenore Berger Bingham and her family, with gratitude for always encouraging me to express myself.

by Kelly, 9

Copyright © 2005 by Joyce Raimondo

First published in 2005 by Watson-Guptill Publications
A division of VNU Business Media, Inc.
770 Broadway, New York, NY 10003
www.wgpub.com

Step-by-step artwork by Joyce Raimondo. Photography of three-dimensional children's art by Frank Roccanova.

Picture credits: Page 9: *The Scream* by Edvard Munch. © 2004 The Munch Museum/The Munch-Ellingsen Group/Artists Rights Society (ARS), NY. Image © National Gallery, Norway. Photograph: J. Lathion. Cover and Page 15: *The Starry Night* by Vincent van Gogh. Digital image © The Museum of Modern Art/Licensed by SCALA/Art Resource, New York. Page 21: *Street, Dresden* by Ernst Ludwig Kirchner. Digital image © The Museum of Modern Art/Licensed by SCALA/Art Resource, NY. Image © by Ingeborg and Dr. Wolfgang Henze-Ketterer, Wichtrach/Bern. Page 29: *Klamm Improvisation* by Vasily Kandinsky. © Städtische Galerie im Lenbachhaus, Munich. Page 35: *Woman V* by Willem de Kooning. © 2004 The Willem de Kooning Foundation/Artists Rights Society (ARS), New York. Page 41: *Convergence: Number 10* by Jackson Pollock. © 2004 The Pollock-Krasner Foundation/Artists Rights Society (ARS), New York.

Every effort has been made to ensure accuracy in this book and to acknowledge all copyright holders. We will be pleased to correct any inadvertent errors or omissions in future editions.

Library of Congress Cataloging-in-Publication Data

Raimondo, Joyce.
  Express yourself! : activities and adventures in expressionism / by Joyce Raimondo.
     p. cm. — (Art explorers ; 3)
  ISBN 0-8230-2506-3 (hc) ; ISBN 0-8230-2492-X (pbk)
  1. Expressionism (Art)—Juvenile literature. 2. Art—Study and teaching (Primary)—Activity programs. I. Title.
  N6494.E9R35 2005
  372.5—dc22

                              2005008257

Senior Acquisitions Editor: Julie Mazur
Project Editor: Audrey Walen
Designer: Edward Miller
Production Manager: Ellen Greene
The typefaces in this book include Futura, Typography of Coop, and Ad Lib.

Manufactured in the Singapore

First printing, 2005

by Lucy, 9

Contents

by Camila, 9

Note to Adults: Help Your Child Explore Expressionism 4
Note to Kids: Express Yourself! 6

Picture Your Feelings—Edvard Munch 8
    Who's Afraid? 10
    Print It Out! 12

Moody Places—Vincent van Gogh 14
    If Skies Could Talk 16
    Lively Lines 18

Go Wild With Color—Ernst Ludwig Kirchner 20
    Color the City 22
    Face It! 24
    Mask Believe 26

Amazing Abstract Art—Vasily Kandinsky 28
    Sensational Shapes 30
    Movement and You 32

Emotions in Action—Willem de Kooning 34
    Gooey Glorious Paint 36
    Sculpt It Out! 38

Let It Flow!—Jackson Pollock 40
    Drip It! Pour It! Squirt It Out! 42
    Collect It! Collage It! 44

Artist Biographies 46
About the Author 48
Acknowledgments 48

by Yancy, 9

Help Your Child Explore Expressionism

Express Yourself! invites children to enter the world of expressionism and utilize it as a **springboard for their own creativity.** The discussions in this book encourage children to **examine** works of art and **develop their own personal interpretations.** Related projects, inspired by the artists, guide children on a journey of self-expression.

What do you see in this picture?

The expressionists wanted to convey their inner life and emotions in art. Looking at their pictures, you might identify with the dramatic subjects and strong feelings they express. The questions in this book **motivate creative thinking** by asking children to describe and interpret these paintings. Let go of your own ideas about what the artwork means, and affirm the children's insights. In a group, **encourage different opinions.** Ask children to go further with their ideas. Older children may want to research the artists' lives, and they can start with the brief biographies in this book.

Express Your Feelings

Some expressionists painted their emotions by portraying dramatic images— landscapes, cityscapes, and people—with dazzling colors and brushstrokes. Others expressed their inner life through vibrant abstract art. *Express Yourself!* invites children to do the same—**to express their feelings through art.** Some of the projects ask children to try working with the working methods of the artists, such as drip painting or using pure colors. Other projects **explore expressionist concepts** with materials adapted for children—for example, children make colorful masks inspired by the artist Ernst Ludwig Kirchner.

Everyone Is Creative

The instructions in this book guide young artists on a **journey of self-discovery.** Do not expect children to follow them exactly. Begin with a lively conversation to **spark ideas.** For example, when discussing Edvard Munch's *The Scream,* ask children what frightens them and have them paint their fears. Demonstrate techniques, such as how to draw a

by Paulina, 9

4

feeling face. Sometimes it is helpful to let children **play with the materials,** making brushstrokes or mixing colors on a separate sheet of paper before they begin the project. Encourage children to work with a spirit of **experimentation.**

Keep in mind that **everyone has his or her own way of expressing emotions** and there is no one formula for communicating emotions in art. For example, to one child blue might be sad, while to another it might be calm or relaxing. Remember to encourage children to express the full range of their feelings—anger, joy, fear, sadness, silliness—in art. Celebrate the unique ideas of each child— **creativity is a gift to be nurtured in everyone.**

by Kassandra, 11

Expressionism and the Art of Inner Life

Expressionism is a current in modern art that spreads across many countries and encompasses a variety of styles and techniques. Rather than paint outward appearances, expressionist artists turn inward, painting according to their own subjective psychological impulses. This book highlights five revolutionary artists who expressed their spiritual and emotional worlds through exaggerated images of people and places—or through purely abstract painting—using suggestive colors, shapes, and lines.

Two early expressionists, Vincent van Gogh and Edvard Munch, created a radical new art—portraying highly dramatic subjects with intense colors, dynamic brushstrokes, and distorted forms. A second wave of expressionism took root in Dresden, Germany, from 1905–13, with the founding of the group Die Brücke (The Bridge). Led by Ernst Ludwig Kirchner, these artists reacted against established academic art and the social order, seeking freedom to communicate their individuality. Psychologically charged, they used clashing colors, hard-edged forms, and bold outlines to express their inner conflicts and the anxieties of modern life. In Munich, the artists' group Der Blaue Reiter (The Blue Rider), founded by Vasily Kandinsky and Franz Marc in 1911, used imagination and spirituality as a source of inspiration. Kandinsky captured his inner world and spiritual life in vibrant abstract paintings. The German Expressionist groups disbanded with the onset of World War I. In the 1930s many of their works were removed from museums and confiscated by the Nazis. Despite such opposition, the German Expressionists opened doors for generations of modern artists worldwide to explore their own creativity.

Drawing upon the expressionist emphasis on individuality, Abstract Expressionism evolved in the United States from 1945–60 with two leading figures, Jackson Pollock and Willem de Kooning. For these artists, the physical act of painting itself—the flow and energy of color and paint—became a dynamic means of expression. Exploring exuberant gestures and movements, they became known as "action painters."

Each of the artists in this book courageously followed his own vision. Some achieved fame in their lifetimes, while others, such as van Gogh, sold only one painting. By following their own approaches to art making, they inspire us to seek out personal ways to express ourselves—however different or unconventional we might be.

Express Yourself!

What happens to you when you are **happy?** Do you jump up in the air or dance all around? What do you do when you are **angry** or **sad?** Do you frown or cry or shout out loud? How do you look when you are **surprised** or **scared?** Does your mouth open wide as you let out a yell? **Express yourself!** Take the **feelings** and **thoughts** that are **inside** of you, and show them on the **outside.** Draw a **picture,** write a **poem,** make a **face,** sing a **song,** or **talk** about how you feel.

This book invites you to **express your feelings in art.** Start by looking at paintings by famous **expressionist** artists. The expressionists painted **people** and **places** using **exaggeration** and **bold colors** to get their feelings across. In their pictures, you might find a sad woman whose face is green or a frightened man screaming with a gigantic wide-open mouth. You will see an exciting windy sky with stars so bright they explode like fireworks in the night.

You will also discover how **abstract** artists painted their feelings with **lines, shapes,** and **colors.** Whirling lines might remind you of a crazy storm or

So silly.—Rienna, 9

the joyful movement of waves and wind. A burst of yellow might remind you of a happy day.

You will also learn how the **Abstract Expressionists** invented fun ways of using paint that you can also use to **get your energy and emotions out.** Dip a stick into a cup of paint, and **drip** it all around. **Swoosh** colors together. **Scratch** into your paint to release anger. Or, in a lively dance, move your body as you paint. Discover the **exciting things that paint can do.**

Some of the paintings in this book might look **messy** or **funny** or **different** from anything you have ever seen. Long ago, some people thought this art was frightening or ugly. But, no matter what, the artists painted in their own ways. Today, they are known as **great artists.**

See for yourself. **Look** at their pictures. Then **create your own art.** Print a feeling face, or make a colorful mask. Sculpt a person out of clay, or paint a moody sky. You can express any feeling in art, even scary or sad ones. Your art can be as **strange** or **unique** as you want it to be. Picture how you feel—and **let your imagination run free.**

Confusion.—Nicole, 11

PICTURE YOUR FEELINGS

EDVARD MUNCH

Edvard Munch expressed all of his feelings and memories in his art—even the scary ones. Like a nightmare, everything in this picture is frightening. Eyes staring and mouth wide open, the person looks shocked as he covers his ears. Can you imagine what he is hearing and seeing? In the distance, two mysterious men seem to follow him. Look into the background. The person is surrounded by blackness against a spooky red-orange sky. Wavy lines swirl all around. It is as if you can hear a loud scream echoing through the picture.

Munch got his idea for *The Scream* one evening as he was walking on a road along the water. He felt tired and ill. The sun was setting and the sky was bright red. Later, the artist wrote in his diary, "I felt as though a scream went through nature . . . . I painted this picture . . . the colors were screaming." Munch did not explain exactly why the person is screaming. He left it up to us to create our own scary tale.

How does this person feel? How can you tell?

- What does his **face** show? What is **unusual** about it? Notice the way the **hands** are **covering his ears.** Why do you think that is? What do you notice about his **body**?
- **Who** is this? What is he **doing**?
- Look closely, can you find two other **people** in this scene? What are they **doing** there? **Who** are they?
- **Where** is this? How would you describe this **place**?
- What do you notice about the **sky**? What **time of day or night** is it? Notice all of the **swirling lines** in the picture. What do they show?
- Look at the **colors**. What **mood** do they show?

The Scream, 1893
tempera and oil pastel on
cardboard, 35 7/8 x 29 inches
(91 x 73 1/2 cm)
National Gallery, Norway

- The artist, Munch, used exaggeration to show how the person feels. What in the picture looks **exaggerated** or **unreal**?
- The name of the painting is **The Scream**. What in the picture tells us the person is screaming? What is he **screaming** about? Why is he so **frightened or surprised**?

What do you think will happen next? Write a story about the man in this picture.

What frightens you? What makes you happy or sad or angry? The art projects in this section invite you to tell stories about your feelings in pictures.

9

Who's Afraid?

Make a painting of something that frightens you.

What are you afraid of? Monsters under your bed? Giant spiders? Fast roller coasters? Like Munch, paint a person screaming or shivering in fright. Then, show why the person is scared. You can paint something real or imaginary.

1. First, draw yourself. Think about the way your body looks when you are frightened. For example, I drew myself running with my hands in the air. You can also draw yourself shivering or holding yourself for protection. (Draw simple large shapes so it will be easy to paint.)

2. Draw a frightened face. I drew a wide-open mouth because I am screaming and surprised. I made big eyes to show I am in shock. (If you want, you can wait for your painting to dry, and draw the features of the face later.)

3. Add hair. Have it stand straight up in the air or wave around to show fear.

4. Show what you are scared about. I am afraid of getting knocked over by a giant wave when I swim in the ocean. I call my picture *Look Out – Here Comes a Big One!* You might draw green ghosts, barking dogs, dragons, or anything that scares you.

5. Paint bold brushstrokes that swirl around your picture to create a frightening look. You can also choose colors that look scary.

6. Wait for your painting to dry. Then, add crayon lines—swirling, jittery, or nervous—to get a scary feeling across. You can also add details and draw outlines in your picture.

7. Talk about it. Tell an adult or a friend what your picture is about.

I thought I heard a scream. I painted this picture. . .the colors were screaming.—Edvard Munch

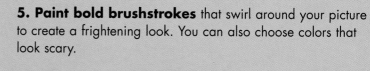

Supplies

Paper	Crayons
Paint	Water
Brushes	Sponges to
Palette	clean brushes

Giant insects! —Alana, 11

Zooming on a roller coaster! —Nadia, 9

Aliens are landing! —Joseph, 10

Picture Your Memories

Munch painted all the memories of his life, even the sad ones. Once he painted a picture of his sister when she was sick in bed. Draw a picture that tells about a memory when you felt really happy or sad. Show how you felt and what was happening. For example, draw yourself smiling at your birthday party with presents, friends, and a cake. Or, you might draw the sad day your friend moved away. Like Munch, you can write about your memories in a journal, too.

Happy birthday! —Cristina, 6

Waving goodbye to my friend.
—JoJo, 6

Print It Out!

Create a feeling face using Styrofoam printmaking.

In addition to painting, Munch made a **printed woodcut** of *The Scream* with bold black ink. (A **print** is made when you make a copy of your artwork.) Like Munch, make a print that shows a dramatic facial expression. This project shows you an easy printmaking method that you can do at home.

1. Sketch faces that show feelings to get ideas. Exaggerate the facial features. In Munch's picture, the frightened face has a huge open mouth. You might make a happy face with a gigantic smile or sad face with really big teardrops. Choose an idea for your print.

2. Make the printing plate out of Styrofoam. You can buy Styrofoam sheets from an art supply store, or cut a flat rectangle out of a disposable Styrofoam dish.

3. Press lines into the Styrofoam with a pencil to create a face. Notice how the lines are actually carved into the sheet. (If you press too lightly, your picture will not show up.) Draw simple shapes and lines; details that are too tiny will not work. Do not write words—they will print backwards.

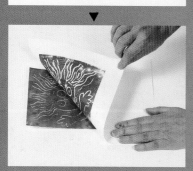

4. Roll ink onto the Styrofoam with a brayer (roller). Start at the top, and roll carefully. Try to get an even coat of ink. Notice how the lines show up white! (Tip: Do not put too much ink on your brayer; it will fill up the lines.)

5. Place a sheet of paper over the Styrofoam. Gently rub the paper and press on it with your hand or a clean brayer.

6. Surprise! Lift up the paper to see your print.

7. Copy it! Repeat the process to print more pictures. Experiment. Roll out more than one color ink to make a rainbow print. Try printing on different types of paper.

Supplies

Water-based printing ink
Brayer (roller)
Paper
Pencil
Styrofoam sheet

Oh, no!—Sarah, 8

Print into Collage

Make a colorful **collage** by gluing down colored tissue paper shapes. Make sure they are glued flat, and let them dry. Then, print a face right over your collage. The colors of your collage will show through the ink! You can choose colors that show the feeling of the face. For example, for a sad face you might glue blue and gray tissue paper. For an excited face, you might use yellow and red papers.

A puzzled look.—Sarah, 10

Stunned and startled.—Jessie, 8

Weeping girl.—Claudia, 9

Steam coming out of my ears.—Max, 8

MOODY PLACES

VINCENT VAN GOGH

One morning Vincent van Gogh woke up early before the sun had risen. He looked out his window in France. The sky was still dark except for a morning star shining brightly. Van Gogh once said, "Looking at the stars always makes me dream." Inspired, he painted *The Starry Night*. Instead of painting the sky exactly as it looks in real life, van Gogh filled his picture with imagination and emotion.

Everything in this scene expresses a feeling. Look into the swirling blue brush-strokes in the sky. The wind seems to be whirling with excitement. The bright stars look like fireworks bursting in the night. Below the dazzling sky, van Gogh painted a calm, quiet town. In the center, he added a peaceful church that he remembered from his homeland, Holland. Can you find the steeple? Can you find trees that reach upward like flames? Full of movement and energy, van Gogh's painting is turbulent, hopeful, and alive!

If you could float up in this sky, what would that be like? What would you see?

- What time of **day or night** is it? How can you tell?
- Notice all the **swirls**. What do they tell you about the **weather**?
- What **feeling** does the sky have? What about it seems **exciting**? What other words **describe** it?
- Look at the **place** below. **Where** is this? What **mood** does this place have? Is it calm or active, quiet or loud? What other words would you use?
- Travel to the **background** near the town. Notice those **blue curving lines** behind it. What could those be?
- Look at the **trees**. How would you **describe** them? Find a **church**. What else do you see?

14

The Starry Night, 1889
oil on canvas, 29 x 36 ¼ inches (73.7 x 92.1 cm)
Acquired through the Lillie P. Bliss Bequest.
The Museum of Modern Art, New York

- Look at all the **lines** and **brushstrokes**. Can you find **curves** and **dashes** and **straight lines**? What **patterns** do you see?
- Notice the **colors**. How many different kinds of **blues** do you see? What **mood** do the colors create?
- Think about the way the sky usually looks. What in van Gogh's picture looks **make-believe**?

Compare the starry sky in this painting to the one in Munch's picture on page 9. How are they different or similar?

How do you feel when you look at the sky outside your window?
The art projects in this section invite you to paint places that are filled with feeling.

15

If Skies Could Talk

Paint a sky that shows an emotion.

Sometimes when the sun is shining, we feel happy. When it rains, we might be sad. A thunderstorm sounds like the sky is really mad. In van Gogh's painting, the windy sky is filled with excitement. Like van Gogh, paint a picture of a sky that shows a feeling. Use lively brushstrokes and bold colors to capture the weather.

▼

▼

1. Experiment! Before you begin your picture, make all kinds of brushstrokes on scrap paper. For example, paint dots, dashes, swirls, and straight lines.

2. What weather will you paint? What mood will you show? Here are some ideas: an angry thunderstorm, a sad rainy day, a hopeful sunrise, a joyful rainbow, an excited storm, a wild tornado, a peaceful night sky.

3. Sketch with simple shapes. I drew clouds and a rainbow with the ocean below. What will you put in your sky—a sun, a moon, lightning, a star, or something else? Choose a place to add to your picture. You might draw mountains, a forest, a village, a garden, or another place.

4. Brush it on! Instead of filling the sky with one solid color, paint it with brushstrokes. Like van Gogh, show the movement of the weather. I painted swirling wind and dashes of rain to show an excited storm. You can use zigzags for lightning, dashes of yellow for rays of sun, or spirals for a tornado.

5. Color a moody sky. I mixed blues to show the feeling of a cold, stormy sky. My yellow sun and rainbow show happiness peeking through the storm. You can use dark colors for a gloomy mood. Or, use yellows, oranges, and reds for a glowing sunrise.

6. Paint the place below. Look at my exciting ocean filled with whirling waves of blue. You can paint calm green rolling hills, angry rock mountains, a lively city skyline, or any place you can imagine.

7. Add details. When your painting dries, you can paint a person with the same mood as the place. Add details such as trees, flowers, and windows.

Supplies

Paper
Paint
Brushes
Palette
Water
Sponges to
    clean brushes

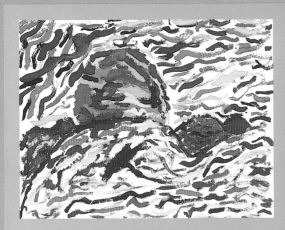

Try these, too!

Feeling Warm

In many of van Gogh's pictures, the warm sun shines on golden land or bright yellow stars glow with happiness in the dark. What feeling does yellow suggest to you? Make a picture filled mostly with **warm colors** by mixing yellows, oranges, reds, and white. You might paint a field of sunflowers bursting with joy or a golden meadow.

Hot sunshine makes me happy.
—Valerie, 10

Feeling Cool

Instead of painting the night black, van Gogh mixed beautiful blues and greens for *The Starry Night*. Like van Gogh, paint a place with **cool colors.** Mix blues, purples, greens, and white. Show a feeling. For example, you might paint a calm blue sea, a freezing winter storm, or a sad rainy day.

Feeling blue on a rainy day.
—Connor, 11

Angry as lightning!—Jillian, 11

A joyful sunrise.—Briana, 6

Tears cry over the city.—Joseph, 6

Lively Lines

Another van Gogh idea

Make a picture of a moody place with markers and watercolor.
Instead of painting everything with outlines, van Gogh filled his pictures with lively lines and patterns. In *The Starry Night,* swirling curves capture the wind. Stars whirl with dashes of color. In addition to painting, van Gogh made many line drawings of the countryside using a reed pen that he dipped in ink. Try it yourself. Make a line drawing, then paint it.

▼

▼

1. Draw different kinds of lines on scrap paper before you begin your picture. Draw with the tip of your marker for thin lines and the side of it for thicker ones. Make dots, dashes, squiggles, and curls. Can you make lines that look nervous, angry, silly, happy, or sad?

2. Choose a place for your picture. What kind of feeling will you show? I drew a peaceful countryside. You might draw a spooky forest, a fun ocean, a relaxing tropical island, or an exciting city. Think about what you might find there, such as trees, roads, flowers, or buildings.

3. Draw lines to show the movement and feeling of the place. I drew curvy rolling hills and wavy lines to show a soft breeze. Dashes and dots show rays of the sun. You can draw a spooky forest with shaky lines for branches and tangled spiderwebs. You might draw curls to show an ocean wind and waves.

4. Draw patterns. (A pattern is made when you repeat the same line or shape over and over.) Notice the lines of grass and trees that repeat in my picture. You can make spirals of wind that dance across your paper, a star-spangled sky, or ocean waves that make a lively pattern.

5. Add watercolor paint.
Do not just fill in the shapes. Instead, paint over the lines of your drawing. You can also make new patterns and lines with your watercolor brush. I had fun making blades of grass and swirls of sunshine with my brush.

Supplies

Paper
Watercolor paint
Brushes
Permanent markers
   (non-water soluble)
Water
Sponges to clean
   brushes

Cool breeze by the sea.—Amanda, 8

The wild forest.—Daniel, 8

Volcano, tornado, meteors, and lightning.—Dominic, 9

Try this, too!

Exciting fireworks.—Sonia, 8

I often think the night is more alive and more richly colored than the day. —Vincent van Gogh

Out of Darkness

Van Gogh saw vibrant color everywhere, even in the dark. In *The Starry Night*, bright rays of light shine from the moon and stars explode like fireworks. What colors do you see at night? Paint a moody night sky filled with light using bright colored paints on black paper. Use thick brushstrokes. Think about the feeling and movement of the lines as you paint. Are they calm, stormy, excited, or cheerful?

GO WILD WITH COLOR

ERNST LUDWIG KIRCHNER

Imagine a place where sidewalks are pink and people have green faces! That's what the artist Ernst Ludwig Kirchner did when he painted this street scene. Kirchner lived in the big city of Dresden, Germany. Instead of painting his city with ordinary gray sidewalks and normal-looking people, Kirchner changed the colors of things to express his feelings. In his picture, he captured the hustle and bustle of a crowded city. Colorful women dressed in fancy gowns and hats stroll down the street. Their strange orange and green faces stare with blank expressions. A little girl dressed in black seems to be lost in the crowd. Even though there are many people, no one seems to be looking at each other or talking to anyone else.

Kirchner once said that he felt alone when he was in a crowd. Some people think this colorful scene looks frightening and lonely. Others see it as a lively masquerade. What do you think?

Imagine yourself in this crowd. What would that be like?

- Notice the two **women**—one has a **green face**, another is **orange**! Why would that be? What **feelings** do their faces show? What else seems to be **strange** about them?
- What do you notice about the way people are **dressed**? What does that tell you?
- Find a little **girl**. How do you think she **feels**? What is she **doing** there? What is she **holding** in her hand? What else do you notice about her?
- **Where** are all these **people**? What are they **doing**? What gives you that idea?

STREET, DRESDEN, 1908
oil on canvas, 59 ¼ x 78 ⅞ inches
(150.5 x 200.4 cm)
Collection of The Museum of Modern Art, New York

- None of the people seem to be **looking at each other**. Why would that be? Imagine what they are all looking at.
- Is this scene taking place **now** or **a long time ago**? How can you tell?
- Look into the **background**. Find a **red rectangular shape**. What could that be?
- How would you describe the **colors** in this picture? Which seem **strange** or **make-believe**? What **mood** do the colors give?

Would you want to be in this picture? Why or why not?

Color your world! The art projects in this section invite you to express your feelings with bright, bold colors of paint.

Color the City

Make art inspired by Kirchner

Make a picture of a city street in colors that capture your feelings.
Have you ever visited the city? Do you live in one? Think about the normal colors of city streets, buildings, cars, and people. Then use your imagination. Like Kirchner, paint a city where everything is colored to fit your mood. On a sad day, people are blue and the sky is dark gray. On a happy day, buildings are rainbow colors and people walk on yellow streets!

1. Play with your oil pastels on a piece of scrap paper before you begin your picture. You can draw one color over another to create new ones. Blend and smear colors together with a paper towel. Use the end of a paintbrush to scratch lines into the oil pastels. Try these techniques in your picture.

2. Choose a mood for your city picture. Here are some ideas: silly city, scary town, love street, dulls-ville, sad place.

3. Make your drawing. Start with a line for the street. Then, add people. Invent new colors for things. I drew a lady with blue hair and a purple eye!

4. Draw colorful buildings and other details. I drew tall skyscrapers with rainbow-colored windows. Add other things such as cars, taxis, buses, streetlights, or anything else.

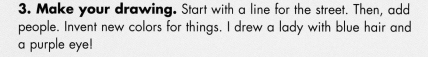

5. What do you imagine in the sky? Mix up the colors. In my silly picture, I painted the sky green! In scary town, you might paint a black sun. On love street, you could paint puffy pink clouds!

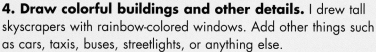

6. Paint in your picture. Change the colors of everything to show a feeling. I made a silly city filled with funny colors. Look at the man with the green face and blue lips! In scary town, you might color everything orange and black like Halloween. On love street, you could paint hot pink buildings and red roads!

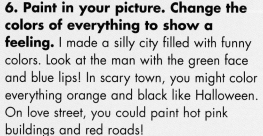

7. Add finishing touches. When your painting dries, you can draw back in details such as lips and eyes with oil pastels. You can also draw bold outlines if you like.

Supplies

Oil pastels
Paper
Paint
Brushes
Water
Sponges to clean
    brushes

Gloomy town.—Arousiah, 10

Fantasy New York.—Ally, 11

Disco dance city.—Alejandro, 10

Try this, too!

Color the Countryside

When Kirchner was older he moved to the mountains in Switzerland. He filled his paintings with imaginative bright colors to show the peace in the countryside. In his pictures, you can see pink mountaintops and green skies! Have you ever gone on a drive through the country? Paint a landscape. Change the colors of the world—let your imagination run free. Why not paint a pink tree and bright blue grass!

Look! It's a rainbow sky!—Philip, 9

Face It!

Paint a face that shows a feeling using bold colors.

A woman with a green face! How could that be? Instead of painting normal skin colors, Kirchner and his artist friends painted with wild colors to express feelings. They believed every artist should have the freedom to paint in his or her own way. In their pictures, you might see a sad girl with a blue face or an angry man with red eyes. Try it yourself!

1. Make faces! To get ideas, play a guessing game. Write feeling words on index cards, such as happy, sad, mad, confused, frustrated, and shocked. Pick a card, and act the feeling out with your face. See if your friends can guess it. If you are by yourself, look in the mirror and practice making faces. **Then, choose a facial expression for your picture.**

2. Paint with pure colors. For this project, don't mix colors. Instead, paint a face with the bright colors of the rainbow—red, orange, yellow, green, blue, purple. You can also use black for bold outlines, if you want. (Clean off your paintbrush each time you dip into a new color, or use a different brush for each color.)

3. Paint an oval for the face. Add eyes, mouth, ears, nose, and other details to show a feeling. For example, big yellow eyes with orange circles around them might show surprise. To show anger, I made red eyeballs with thick eyebrows pointing into them.

4. Color in the skin. Do not paint realistic-looking skin color. Instead, paint colors to show an emotion. I painted a red, furious face with a green forehead! A blue face might be sad. You can also make a multi-colored face that is silly or strange.

5. What feeling does the hair show? I made spiky orange hair for excitement and anger. Curly rainbow-colored hair might look happy or silly.

6. Paint in the background.
Fill it with colorful designs if you like.

Supplies

Paper
Paint
Brushes
Palette
Water
Sponges to clean brushes

My goal was always to express emotion and experience with large and simple forms and clear colors.
—Ernst Ludwig Kirchner

Surprise!—Kassandra, 11

The loud scream.—Matthew, 11

Crazy confusion.—Ryan, 10

Try this, too!

Cut Paper Shape Faces

Make a cut-paper **collage** of a face that captures a feeling. First, cut a shape for the face out of construction paper. Then, cut out shapes for the eyes, nose, and mouth that express the emotion you want to show. For example, an angry monster might have black sharp teeth, a green wide-open mouth, and jagged red eyebrows. A silly friend might be made of yellow, pink, and purple curly shapes and squiggles.

The bully next door.—Jessa, 9

Wacky.—Paulina, 9

Mask Believe Fun with faces

Make a colorful mask that expresses an emotion using pâpier maché and paint.

Are the women in Kirchner's painting wearing colorful masks or face paint? Look at the man in Munch's *The Scream* (page 9). Is his face a strange disguise? Kirchner and other modern artists loved to paint funny-looking people whose faces look like mysterious masks. This project invites you to make a mask that you can wear. Have a parade or masquerade party when you are done!

▼

▼

1. Construct a cardboard face. Cut a piece of light cardboard into a rectangle (about 11 x 14 inches). Cut a slit about 3 inches from the top and another one 3 inches from the bottom. Pull the two sides of the top slit together so the shape "pops out." Staple or tape together. Repeat for the bottom slit.

2. Tape on a funny nose. Roll a piece of light cardboard into a tube for a long nose. Or, fold a cardboard triangle in half for a pointed nose.

3. Crumple newspaper into balls for eyes. Then cut cardboard strips for eyebrows to show a feeling. For example, for angry eyes, add eyebrows that are pointing down. For sad eyes, point the eyebrows up. Tape the pieces on.

4. Bend a strip of cardboard for a mouth. Make a big circle for an open mouth that looks surprised. Or, make a big happy smile or a sad frown. Tape it on.

5. Wrap the pâpier maché. Cut a lot of newspaper strips (about 1 inch wide). Prepare wheat paste according to the package directions. Dunk a strip of paper into the wheat paste. Squeeze off excess paste. Wrap the entire mask with pasted strips. Then, add a second layer. (If you do not have wheat paste, use a mixture of white glue and water.)

6. Let the mask dry, then paint it. Use bold colors to express emotion. For example, make a red, angry face or a green, scary face. (For best results, use thick paint.)

Supplies

Light cardboard (oak-tag)
Tape
Wheat paste (buy it at a craft store or hardware store)
Newspaper or newsprint paper strips
Scissors
Paint
Brushes
Water
Sponges to clean brushes

Tired and worried.
—Garbriel, 12

Shocked.
—Hermes, 8

Funny face paint.
—Candice, 9, and
Basil, 9

Fierce face.—Lucas, 8

Try this, too!

Rainbow Faces

Make a colorful tissue-paper mask full of feeling. Cut a shape for the face out of corrugated cardboard or oak-tag. Cut and fold cardboard forms, or crumple newspaper for the eyes, nose, and mouth. Tape them on. Thin out glue by adding water to it. Brush glue onto an area of your mask. Then, place bits of tissue paper down. Continue to wrap the entire cardboard mask with tissue paper pieces. Brush over them with a thin layer of glue. What feeling does your mask show?

Colorful confusion.—Hannah, 9

AMAZING ABSTRACT ART

VASILY KANDINSKY

Instead of painting things the way they look in real life, Vasily Kandinsky painted the world deep inside himself—his imagination, his feelings, and his spirit. What color are thoughts? What color is the feeling you get when you are excited or happy? Can you imagine the world inside your mind?

When Kandinsky painted, he freely invented from his mind, getting ideas as he went along. He once said, "All the forms I ever used . . . created themselves while I was working, often surprising me!" He filled his paintings with exciting lines, shapes, and colors, and he became known as the first abstract artist. Let your eye travel around the colorful swirls and designs. They might remind you of a wild storm or the dizzy feeling you get when you spin round and round. The cool blues and bright yellows might remind you of flowing water and wind on a hot summer day. What do you see?

Imagine how would it feel to be in this painting. What would that feel like?

- Travel in and around this picture. Would it be **exciting**, **confusing**, **scary**, or **fun**? What words would you use to describe it?
- What would the **movement** be like? Would it be calm and slow? Or, topsy-turvy like a twirling, dizzying ride?
- Imagine if the **weather** outside was like this picture. What would that be like?
- If this picture could make **sound**, what kinds of **noises** would you hear coming from it?
- What else does this picture **remind you of**?
- **Look closely**. You might see all kinds of **creatures**. Can you find

Klamm Improvisation, 1914
oil on canvas, 42.9 x 42.9 inches (110 x 110 cm)
Städtische Galerie im Lenbachhaus, Munich

a shape that looks like a **horse** or a **bird**? Can you find lines that look like a **ladder**, a **boat**, a **building**, and a **wave**? Or, do you see something **different**?

* Look at all the **lines** and **shapes**. Can you find **circles** and **curves**? Find **straight** lines and **wavy** ones and **zigzags**. What else do you see?
* What **patterns** do you see? Can you find **stripes** and **dots**?

Look at the entire picture. Make up a title. Why would you call it that?

Make your own abstract picture that shows feelings. The art projects in this section invite you to express your emotions with colors, lines, and shapes.

29

Sensational Shapes

Make an abstract picture that shows an emotion with cut-paper shapes and paint.

Can a shape have a feeling? Look at the swirls and colors that seem to fly across Kandinsky's painting—they might show excitement, a frightening storm, or a fun-filled carnival. Like Kandinsky, make an **abstract** picture that captures an emotion. Fill your picture with lively patterns and designs.

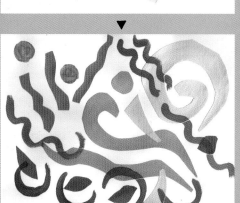

1. What feeling will you show? Choose an emotion for your picture, such as happy, sad, angry, or confused.

2. What shapes remind you of that feeling? Cut them out. I made curvy shapes and spirals to show happiness. Sharp pointy shapes might show anger or fear.

3. Think about the colors you will use. I cut out yellow, orange, and pink to look cheerful. Orange, red, and black might give your picture an angry feeling. Dark blues and grays might look sad and gloomy.

4. Arrange your shapes to show the feeling. My happy shapes seem to float and bounce across the picture. You might show angry shapes colliding into each other in a fight. Confused shapes might go every which way. Glue your shapes down.

5. Paint over and around your shapes. I painted lively patterns and designs. Add new lines and colors. Do not be afraid to change your picture as you work.

6. Title it. What feeling does your picture show?

Supplies

Scissors
Colored paper
Paint
Brushes
Palette
Water
Sponges to
    clean brushes

My silly carnival.—Carina, 11

Frustration.—Alexa, 12

Happy, happy, so happy!—Alisa, 11

Sweet harp song.—Melanie, 8

Try this, too!

Seeing Sound

Did you ever hear a sound that made you jump with fear? Did you ever listen to a song that made you dance all around? Kandinsky wanted to capture sounds in his abstract paintings. His picture might remind you of the sound of wind or all kinds of loud noises. Make your own **abstract** picture that shows sounds with shapes and colors. For example, a big red circle might be a loud sound. A spiral might be a siren. A curving line might be the sound of a flute.

Movement and You

Make an abstract painting that shows movement using watercolor resist.

In Kandinsky's painting, the whirling lines might remind you of a gush of wind in a hurricane or the feeling you get when you are zooming on a crazy roller coaster ride. We are constantly in motion, and everything around us is always moving, too. How do you feel when you are skating on ice or swimming in the ocean? How do you feel when you are flying about in the subway? Show the feeling of movement in an abstract painting.

1. Move about! Make different kinds of movements with your body or your arms. How do you move when you are dancing or spinning or jumping? Can you move like the wind, a rollercoaster, or a tornado?

2. Choose a subject. Here are some ideas: visiting an amusement park, skating on ice, swimming in the ocean, flying in the air, riding on a fast train.

3. Draw lines that show movement with crayon or oil pastels. Draw slowly and press hard. Instead of drawing a picture of yourself in the actual place, draw fun designs and lines that capture the movement. I drew the feeling of an amusement park ride filled with swirling and twirling motions.

4. Make patterns. A pattern is a shape or line that repeats itself over and over. Fill your picture with designs made of dashes, swirls, stripes, and fun shapes. I drew spirals and circles that spin around.

5. Paint it. When your drawing is completed, lightly paint with watercolor over and through the lines. You can add designs and new shapes with the watercolor. Notice how the crayon lines show through the watercolor paint.

Supplies

Crayons or oil pastels
Paper
Watercolor paints
Brushes
Water
Sponges to clean brushes

I love the amusement park.—Tatyana, 10

Back and forth.—Tiffany, 10

Try this, too!

Lines on the Move

Dot, dot, dot! Dash, dash, dash! Curved and twisted, round and round. Draw an abstract picture filled with many different kinds of lines that show movement and feelings. Watch the movement of lines as you draw designs across your paper. Which lines feel happy or calm? Which feel jittery? Which ones remind you of the feeling of wind or a wave or driving on a winding road? Draw with a permanent marker. Then paint your designs with watercolor.

Electric lines.—Chris, 8

Dancing lines.—Desiree, 8

EMOTIONS IN ACTION

WILLEM DE KOONING

Brush it! Smear it! Scrape it! Drip it! As you can see, when Willem de Kooning painted, he was not interested in coloring in the lines. Full of energy, he let the gooey paint smear and colors blend together to release his emotions. At first glance, it might look like de Kooning painted sloppily and carelessly. But he actually stared at his artwork for hours as he painted—painting the surface, scraping the paint away, and then painting again, many times.

De Kooning made a group of six paintings of bold women with strange grins and distorted bodies. He got his idea by looking at ancient figurines and old paintings of women at art museums, and at glamorous models pictured in magazines. Instead of making pictures of pretty girls, de Kooning painted unusual women who are funny, fierce, and full of wild emotion. Some people thought de Kooning's women paintings were ugly, but the artist kept painting his own way, and he became famous for it.

How would you describe this woman?
How do you suppose she feels?

- Look at the **face**. What kind of **expression** does she have? What do you notice about her **eyes**? What does her **mouth** say about her?
- How would you describe her **body**? What about it is **distorted** or **different** from the way people look in real life?
- What **colors** do you see? What **feeling** do the colors give you?
- Look all around the person. What do you see? Can you tell where the person ends and the **background** begins?
- Look at the way the artist used the paint to make this picture. How would you describe that? Can you find any places where the paint is **blended**? **outlined**? **scraped**? **dripped**?

Woman V
1952–53
oil and charcoal on canvas,
60 $^1/_3$ x 44 $^3/_4$ inches
(154.5 x 114.5 cm)
National Gallery
of Australia

- How do you suppose the artist **felt** when he painted this picture? What gives you that idea?
- Imagine. **Why** would an artist paint a picture like this?
- What, if anything, seems **beautiful** about this picture? What about it seems **ugly** to you?
- Choose a **title** for this picture. Why would you call it that?

Think about most pictures of women that you have seen. How is this one different?

Swoosh it! Squeeze It! Paint It! Sculpt it! Get your feelings and energy out by painting, sculpting, and drawing in action.

Gooey, Glorious Paint

Make a painting of a face without using a paintbrush!

When de Kooning painted *Woman V*, he loaded his brush with thick, wet paint and swooshed it around to create this funny-looking woman. Look at her big black eyes and weird smile! Instead of using paintbrushes, make an expressive face by applying paint with things you find around your home. Get your energy and feelings out by scraping into the paint and squishing colors together.

1. Collect things from around your house that you can use to paint. For example, you can apply paint with sponges, a toothbrush, plastic forks and spoons, wooden sticks, cotton balls, rollers, cotton swabs, chopsticks, or cardboard paper towel rolls. Ask an adult to help.

2. Get ready to paint. It is helpful to limit your painting to one of these combinations so the colors don't get muddy—red, purple, and blue *or* yellow, orange, and red *or* blue, green, and purple. Pour your colors on separate spots on a plastic plate. Also use white.

3. Get into it! Cover your paper with paint. Scoop up the paint with one of your tools. I smeared paint on the paper with a sponge. You can also swoosh it all over your paper with a roller or anything else.

4. Paint a shape for the face. I used a stick to make a big oval. What will you use?

5. Add eyes, a nose, and a mouth. Create a feeling for the face. I used the rim of a paper towel roll to make big round eyes. I dabbed the tip of a cotton swab in paint to make dots for the pupils. For the nose, I used a cork. How do you think this girl feels?

6. What can you use to make hair? I smeared on blue paint. Then, I scraped the paint away with a fork. I got my nervous energy out by painting.

7. Swoosh it! Smear it! Mix it! Scrape it! As you paint, move the paint around. Do not be afraid to make a mistake, or change your picture as you go along. Experiment!

Supplies

Objects to paint with (such as sponges, sticks, toothbrush, cotton swabs, roller, plastic fork, and cardboard paper towel rolls)
Paper
Paint
Brushes
Palette
Water
Sponges to clean brushes

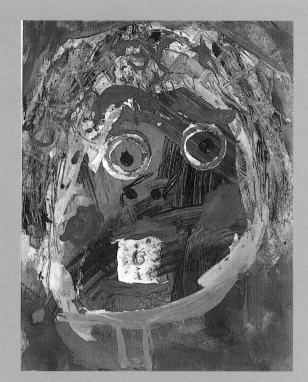

All mixed up.—Justin, 10

Green tears flow.
—Jennifer, 8

Mysterious purple face.—Nitasha, 10

Try these, too!

Play with Paint

Make an abstract painting without using a paintbrush. If you feel mad, you might scrape into the paint with a fork to get your anger out. If you feel nervous, you might make jittery lines with a stick. If you feel sad, you might let watery paint drip all over like tears. Discover the amazing things paint can do. When you are done, give your painting a title.

Action Painting

Work big! Tack a large sheet of paper to the wall. Get large brushes that you might use to paint a house. Sweep the paint across the paper—up, down, and all around. Let it drip and smear. Move your entire body as you paint. This kind of art is called **"action painting."** De Kooning and Jackson Pollock both became famous for it.

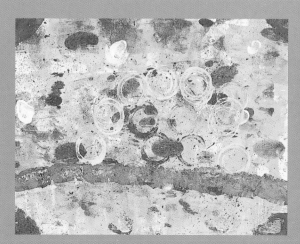

I feel like a glowing sunrise.—Heather, 10

Sculpt It Out!

Make a sculpture inspired by de Kooning

Mold a clay sculpture that expresses a feeling.

In addition to painting, de Kooning made sculptures of people. He squeezed clay, scraped into it, and piled on lumps piece by piece to create figures that are full of feeling. Instead of smoothing out the clay, de Kooning let the imprints of his fingers and the lumpiness of the clay show. Full of the artist's energy, his sculptures capture movement and emotions in action.

1. Squeeze it! Pound it! Rip it! Mush it! Dig your fingers into the clay and play with it. Get your energy out. As you work, you can add pieces of clay to build it up, or squash the clay pieces together. Remove clay by carving it out with tools.

2. Mold it into a person. First, form it into a shape that looks like a big potato. Then, squeeze the clay at the top to form a neck and head. Next, "pull out" the clay to form arms and legs.

3. Pose the body to show a feeling. For example, when you are mad you might stand with your hands on your hips. When you are sad, you might walk with your head down and slump over. I made a person who is cheering with his arms in the air.

4. Squeeze the clay to make a face and other details. Pull out the nose. Push your finger into the face for a mouth. My person has a goofy smile. Also, mold hands and feet.

5. Poke wooden sticks or wires _inside_ the clay to make your sculpture strong. Insert a stick through the head and neck. Push sticks through the arms and legs, attaching them to the body. Also, as you work, do not make clay parts smaller than your pinky finger; they will crack when the clay dries.

6. Push materials into the clay, such as old jewelry, beads, pipe cleaners, and other decorative stuff.

7. When the clay dries, you can paint it. Make it look like a statue with metallic paint. Or, paint a color to show a feeling.

Supplies

Self-hardening clay
Clay tools
Wooden sticks or
  wire pieces
Decorative materials

Hip hip hooray!
—Hermes, 9

I'm scared!
—Raquel, 9

Mad, really mad!
—Timmy, 11

Yikes!
—Raymond, 12

That's what fascinates me
—to make something I
can never be sure of, and
no one else can either. I
will never know, and no
one else will ever know.
That's the way art is.
—Willem de Kooning

Body Talk

De Kooning noticed that people never stand still. He made quick sketches to capture the **gesture,** or movement, of a person. Like de Kooning, use pastels to draw a body in action that shows emotion. You might draw a girl with curling legs dancing with joy. Or, draw an angry muscleman standing with hands on his hips. Smear and blend the pastels to get your feeling across. Press hard on the tip to make bold outlines. Discover what pastels can do.

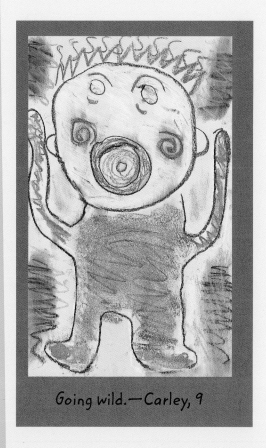

Going wild.—Carley, 9

LET IT FLOW!

JACKSON POLLOCK

Jackson Pollock became famous for an exciting new way of painting called "drip painting." Working in an old barn, he placed a huge canvas on the floor. Then he dipped a stick into a bucket of house paint, and spattered the paint onto his painting. Sometimes he squirted paint from turkey basters or poured it right out of the can! Constantly moving, he walked around all four sides of the painting as he worked. At first glance, it might seem like Pollock was throwing paint in a messy frenzy. But, he actually painted carefully to create beautiful patterns and lines.

   Pollock expressed his feelings in abstract art. You might see an explosion of anger or a tangled web of confusion in his picture. Or, the swirling colors might remind you of a joyful dance and a wild energetic movement. In Pollock's time, some people did not understand his art. Others admired his creativity, and today he is known as one of the greatest American painters.

Look into the swirls of colorful paint. What do you see?

- How do you think the artist **made this picture**? How can you tell?
- What **feelings** does this picture remind you of? Is it **happy, frightening, confusing, angry, messy**, or some other feeling? What gives you that idea?
- What **feeling** do the **colors** give you?
- How would you feel if you were **inside this picture**? What would it be like to **move** through it?
- **Imagine**. You might see make-believe creatures and **animals** and **funny faces**. What else do you see?
- Follow the **lines that flow** around the painting. Can you find any that are **thin** or **thick, curved** or **wiggly**? Can you find any that

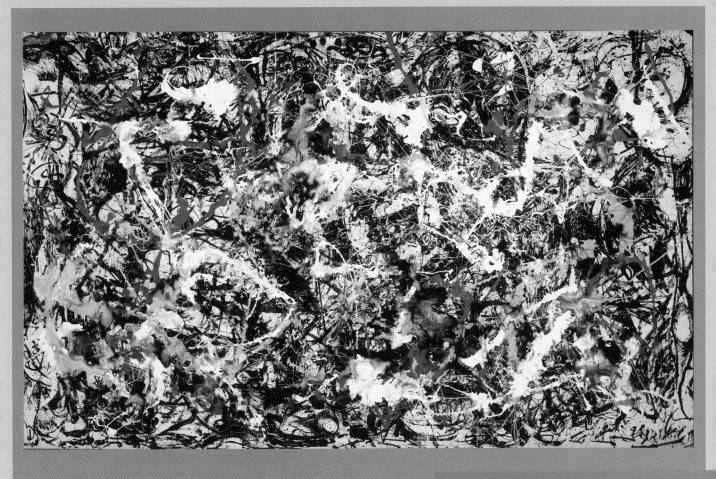

Convergence: Number 10, 1952, 1952
oil on canvas, 93 ¹/₂ x 155 inches (237.5 x 393.7 cm)
Albright-Knox Art Gallery, Buffalo, New York,
Gift of Seymour H. Knox, Jr., 1956

seem to form **letters** of the alphabet?
Do you see any **patterns**?

- How can you tell that this painting was **made on the floor** and not the wall? (Hint—look at the paint drips.)
- Look at the **entire painting**. Make up **a title** for it. Why would you call it that?
- This type of painting is called **"action painting."** What kind of action or **movement** do you see in it?

Think about most pictures you have seen.
How is this one different?

Drip It! Pour It! The art projects in this section invite you to release your feelings as you spatter paint in the spirit of Pollock.

Drip It! Pour It! Squirt It Out!

Make a "drip painting" that expresses a feeling.

Instead of painting a picture of a face or a person, Pollock expressed his feelings by dripping paint in an energetic web of movement. The yellow, orange, and black spatters might show anger or fear. The swirling lines might remind you of exciting fireworks exploding or a bunch of crazy, mixed-up thoughts. Try it yourself!

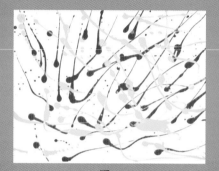

▼

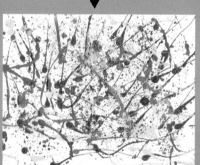

▼

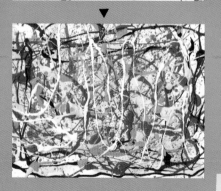

1. Paint on the ground! Roll out a large sheet of postal paper on the floor or outside. Hold the paper down with tape or heavy objects such as rocks. Or, use a small sheet of paper on a table.

2. Get set up. Fill cups or small buckets with paint colors. You might add water to thin it out. Get wooden sticks from the hardware or paint store. Or, use Popsicle sticks or paintbrushes. Gather other fun things to paint with such as basters and spray bottles.

3. Drip it! Dip your stick into the paint, then spatter it onto your painting. As you paint, move around the painting with your entire body. Flick the paint really hard. Or, let it flow into smooth thin lines.

4. Like Pollock, squirt paint out of a baster. Or, use a spray bottle, mustard dispenser, or even a water pistol. (For safety, always aim at your paper, not at people.)

5. Experiment! Invent your own ways of applying paint. Dunk a marble or ball into paint, and roll it onto your paper. Blow through a straw and watch the paint move. You can even pour paint right out of the bucket or bottle. **Splat!**

6. Show a feeling. In my painting, bright colors remind me of a happy spring day. Thick spatters of red and black can show anger. Wavy blue lines might remind you of a calm sea.

7. Title your painting. I call mine *Joyful Springtime*.

Supplies

Roll of postal wrap or large sheets of paper
Tempera paint in cups or buckets
Sticks or brushes
Painting "tools" such as basters, spray bottles, balls
Water
Sponges to clean painting tools

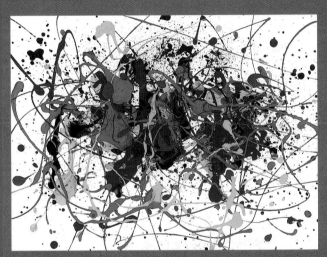

Get your anger out! —Elyse, 9

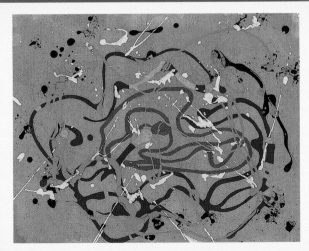

Fun-filled dance of paint. —Rachael, 9

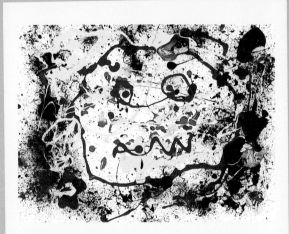

I see a funny face. —Jimmy, 12

Smooth and relaxing. —Darren, 12

Try these, too!

Hands-on

Pollock once said that he wanted to feel as if he was *in* the painting as he worked. Sometimes he actually walked right onto the painting. At other times, he pressed his hands into the painting, leaving behind handprints. Brush water-based paint onto your hands, and press your hands onto the paper. Wash your hands, then drip and spatter paint. How does that feel?

Drawing in Air

In some of Pollock's paintings the wild drips form strange creatures, energetic wiggly people, and funny faces. Surprise yourself! Drip paint, and then look for faces or creatures in it. Or, purposely spatter paint or squeeze it from a mustard dispenser to create a picture of a face, person, or animal that's filled with energy and emotion.

Collect It! Collage It!

Make a collage drip painting that expresses a feeling.

Pollock collected lots of things from around his home, such as pebbles, sand, nails, string, and paper, and added them to his artwork. Sometimes he stuck the materials right into his drips of paint, or glued them on before painting. The materials added **texture**—a rough, smooth, bumpy, or shiny feel—to his paintings. This kind of artwork—when you glue materials to a flat surface—is called a **collage**.

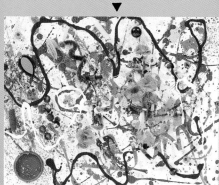

Supplies

Heavy paper or board
Collage materials
Glue
Scissors
Paint in cups or buckets
Sticks or brushes
Water
Sponges to clean brushes

1. Choose a feeling or theme for your collage. Here are some ideas: a happy party, a stormy ocean, a spooky Halloween, a cheerful garden. Or, start working without a subject in mind and think about what your collage expresses when you are done.

2. Collect materials from around your house. I gathered pipe-cleaners, beads, flowers, ribbon, and scraps of wrapping paper to show a happy party. For an ocean theme, you can collect seashells, sand, pebbles, and blue strings. For a scary feeling, you might cut up orange and black papers.

3. Glue materials in an abstract design to capture a feeling. For example, I did not draw people and presents, instead I glued colorful stuff floating around to show the feeling of a party. (For heavy objects, such as seashells, pipe cleaners, or plastic items, ask an adult to glue them for you with a hot-glue gun.)

4. Drip paint over your collage. You can choose colors that fit your subject. I spattered bright yellows, oranges, pinks, and reds. What colors will you use?

5. Sprinkle it! While the paint is wet, you can sprinkle sand, glitter, or sequins into it. You can also glue more things to it after it dries.

6. Title your artwork. Ask people what feeling they think your artwork shows. I call mine *Wild Party*.

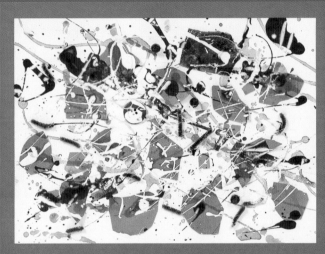

The feeling of Halloween.—Evelyn, 10

Go wild!—Melissa, 12, and Miranda, 11

Crazy Cutouts

Cut it up! Sometimes Pollock cut out shapes from his spattered paintings. Make a drip painting, and let it dry. Then, cut out shapes for people, animals, or anything else from the dried painting. Paste the spattered shapes to a plain background or onto another drip painting.

Wild winter storm.—Keith, 9

Rip It Up!

Pollock married the painter Lee Krasner, who also invented exciting ways of making art. Sometimes Krasner tore up her own paintings! Then, she rearranged the ripped-up pieces to create a new picture. Looking at her **abstract collages**, you might see excitement or anger or joy. Like Krasner, make a painting, and then rip it into shapes. Glue the torn pieces in a whole new way onto another sheet of paper. Then add more paint. What does your painting express?

Spring is here!—Vicky, 9

Artist Biographies

Edvard Munch
Norwegian, 1863–1944

Edvard Munch was raised in Oslo (then called Christiana) in Norway. When he was a child, his mother and one of his sisters died. His father became depressed, and his older sister took over the household. As a young man, first he followed his father's advice and studied engineering, but shortly after he entered art school. Munch told about the painful memories of his childhood in his art. Some people did not like the scary subjects and strong emotions in his paintings, and his art often caused an uproar. Later, Munch began painting landscapes and portraits, and his work began to sell. In 1889, he had his first one-person exhibition, and won a state prize to study art in Paris. Throughout his life, Munch traveled to different places—mostly in France, Germany, and Norway—where he exhibited his paintings.

Munch expressed his emotions—joy, sadness, fear, love, and loss—in his art and writing. Everything in his pictures—the bold colors, and dramatic faces and backgrounds—told about feelings. In addition to painting, Munch explored printmaking and photography.

On his 70th birthday, Munch received honors and was recognized as an outstanding artist worldwide. He donated thousands of paintings, prints, drawings, and several sculptures to the city of Oslo, and in 1963, the Munch Museum opened.

Vincent van Gogh
Dutch, 1853–1890

Vincent van Gogh, a son of a preacher, was raised in a village in Holland. When he was 16 he went to work for his uncle who owned an art gallery in London, and later in Paris. He did not do well at his job, and he was fired. Van Gogh was deeply religious, and he applied for a job as a preacher. He moved to a mining town in Belgium so he could help the poor people there. He did not fit in with the other preachers, and he was fired again. Rejected, he moved in with his family, and decided to devote himself to painting.

Van Gogh painted peasants and people at work. Later, he studied art in Paris. His brother Theo, who owned an art gallery, sent him money so he could paint. Van Gogh painted everything around him—the city streets, people, flowers, and his own face—with great imagination and emotion. His paintings are filled with dazzling colors and swirling brushstrokes.

Van Gogh suffered from mental illness and was often hospitalized. In his own lifetime, he only sold one painting. At times, he had no money and barely had enough to eat. No matter what happened, van Gogh painted. Illness overcame him, and he died at age 37. Today his paintings are worth millions of dollars, and he is known as one of the greatest artists of all time.

Ernst Ludwig Kirchner
German, 1880–1938

As a boy, Ernst Ludwig Kirchner took drawing lessons and painted at home. But his family did not want him to become an artist when he grew up, so they sent him to study architecture in the city of Dresden. Kirchner continued painting anyway, and later studied art in Munich.

In 1905, Kirchner and his friends in Dresden formed an artists' group called Die Brücke, German for "The Bridge." They wanted freedom to paint in their own way even if others thought their pictures were ugly. They painted people, the city, and the countryside with unusual colors to express strong emotions. For example, in Kirchner's painting, you might see a sad girl with a green face! The group held exhibitions, and Kirchner wrote about their ideas. In 1911, they moved to Berlin. There, Kirchner started his own art school, but it was not successful. The members began to go their own ways, and in 1913, the group ended.

In 1915, Kirchner was drafted as a soldier in World War I. He became ill, and was forced to leave. Discouraged and sad, he moved to Switzerland to rest and live. There, he painted the peaceful countryside filled with pink mountains and green skies. In addition to painting, Kirchner made prints and sculptures. His bold art has inspired artists worldwide to express feelings in their art. Today, Kirchner is known as a great leader of German Expressionism.

Vasily Kandinsky
Russian, 1866–1944

Vasily Kandinsky grew up wealthy in Odessa, Russia. As a child, he played piano and cello, and painted. At age 20, he studied economics and law in Moscow. When he turned 30, he decided to be a painter, and went to art school in Munich, Germany. Later, he traveled in Europe, painting colorful landscapes. Slowly, his art began to change. Instead of painting people and places, he painted his inner world of imagination and feelings. He also captured music and sounds in abstract paintings.

In 1912, Kandinsky and the artist Franz Marc published *Der Blaue Reiter*, German for "The Blue Rider." This book was filled with essays, music, and pictures that illustrated their new ideas about art. They also organized exhibits of paintings filled with imagination and emotion. In 1914, World War I broke out, and the artists' group, Der Blaue Reiter, ended. Kandinsky returned to Moscow, where he worked toward creating 22 museums, and taught art at the university.

In 1921, Kandinsky moved to Berlin, Germany, where he taught at the Bauhaus, a famous school. When it closed in 1933, he moved to Paris, France. Always exploring, he designed stage scenery, costumes, fabrics, ceramic tiles, furniture, and made prints. Kandinsky is known as a leader of German Expressionism and as the first abstract artist.

Willem de Kooning
Dutch, 1904–1997

Willem de Kooning was born in Rotterdam, Holland. At age 12, he worked for interior decorators and took drawing lessons. Later, he studied painting. At age 22, he moved to America. He painted houses and signs and decorated windows. In the 1930s, he was hired to create murals for a program called the Works Progress Administration. He was paid well and devoted himself entirely to art.

De Kooning painted in his own unique way to release his feelings. In his pictures, you might see a fierce woman with bright pink skin and big eyes popping out of her head. He also made abstract pictures and landscapes with brushstrokes that sweep and swirl across the canvas. De Kooning let the wet paint drip and smear in an energetic motion. During the 1940s and 1950s, de Kooning and his artist friends in New York City discussed ideas about art and exhibited their work. They were called Abstract Expressionists. In 1943, he married the painter and writer Elaine Freid. Some people thought de Kooning's paintings were ugly. But others admired his art, and before long, he became famous.

In 1963, de Kooning bought a country house near the seashore in Springs, Long Island. He captured the light and movement of the beach in abstract paintings. He also began sculpting people in energetic forms. De Kooning lived until age 93. Today, he is known as a great Abstract Expressionist painter.

Jackson Pollock
American, 1912–1956

Jackson Pollock was born in Cody, Wyoming, but grew up in Arizona and California. His family was poor and moved often. Three of Pollock's older brothers were also artists. At age 18, Pollock joined one of his brothers at the Art Students League in New York City. He studied with Thomas Hart Benton. Later, Pollock worked with the Mexican artist David Siqueiros. They experimented with new techniques—pouring and spraying paint onto murals. Pollock began painting the world of his imagination. A weathly art patron, Peggy Guggenheim, gave him an exhibition at her art gallery and paid him a salary so he could spend most of his time painting.

In 1945, Pollock married the artist Lee Krasner. They moved into an old farmhouse in Springs, Long Island. At first, the house had no central heating or plumbing. Times were hard, and Pollock once traded his paintings for groceries. He painted in an old barn in his backyard, where he created his famous "drip paintings." He spattered paint from sticks to create abstract paintings filled with emotion. Pollock's art began to sell and he became famous. Pollock was troubled with depression and alcoholism. At age 44, Pollock died in a car accident. Today his home is a museum, and he is known as a great Abstract Expressionist painter.

About the Author

Joyce Raimondo, creator of the Art Explorer series, is director of Imagine That! Art Education, specializing in helping children access the arts. As a visiting author to schools and a consultant, she teaches children how to look at famous artworks and utilize art history as a springboard for their own creativity. A consultant to the Pollock-Krasner House and Study Center in East Hampton, she develops programs that encourage children to enjoy Abstract Expressionism.

Joyce and Buddy at
Jackson Pollock's house

She is author of The Museum of Modern Art's acclaimed Art Safari series of children's books, kits, and online programs. From 1992–2000, she served as family programs coordinator at MoMA in New York, where she created programs that teach children and adults how to enjoy art.

A painter and sculptor, Joyce Raimondo's illustrations have been featured in such publications as the New York Times and the Boston Globe. Her television appearances include Blue's Clues, Fox Breakfast Time, and NBC News, among others. She divides her time between Manhattan and Amagansett, New York.

Visit her on the web at www.joyceraimondo.com.

Acknowledgments

As director of Imagine That! Art Education, I implement workshops designed to teach children how to enjoy art history. I ask students to describe what they see in famous artworks and follow up with their own creations. Much of the children's art featured in this book was made during these workshops.

A special thanks to the children who contributed artwork: Alana, Alejandro, Alexa, Alisa, Ally, Amanda, Arousiah, Basil, Briana, Candice, Camila, Carina, Carley, Chris, Claudia, Connor, Cristina, Daniel, Darren, Desiree, Dominic, Elyse, Evelyn, Garbriel, Hannah, Heather, Hermes, Jennifer, Jessa, Jessie, Jillian, Jimmy, JoJo (Josephine), Joseph, Justin, Kassandra, Keith, Kelly, Lucas, Lucy, Matthew, Max, Melanie, Melissa, Miranda, Nadia, Nicole, Nitasha, Paulina, Philip, Rachael, Raymond, Rienna, Ryan, Sammy, Sarah (8), Sarah (10), Sonia, Tatyana, Tiffany, Timmy, Valerie, Vicky, and Yancy.

Gratitude is given to my editors, Julie Mazur and Audrey Walen, for bringing clarity to the development of the third volume in the Art Explorers series. I am also thankful to Ed Miller, the designer, who created the book's lively graphics, and to Frank Roccanova, for photography of the children's three-dimensional art.

Grateful acknowledgment is due to the schools whose students participated in this project: Amagansett, Aqueboque, Bridgehampton, Brooklyn Avenue, Project Most (East Hampton), Pulaski Street, Riley Avenue, Roanoke, Southampton, Springs, and Woodward Parkway. Special thanks is given to the art teachers and administrators who arranged the programs: Mary Jane Aceri, Maureen Ahearn, Jane Berzner, Tim Bryden, Nancy Carney, Robin Gianis, Cathleen Goebel, Mary Huysmen, Kathy Lively (PTA), Rebbecca Morgan, Elizabeth Paris, Lois Reboli, Melissa Haupt, Brian Sorrel, and Ricki Weisfelner. Appreciation is given to the Nassau and Suffolk Boards of Cooperative Education who funded many of these workshops. Several of these programs were supported by a grant from New York State Council on the Arts, a state agency, under the auspices of the Pollock-Krasner House and Study Center in East Hampton. I am grateful to Helen Harrison, Director of the Pollock-Krasner House, for her warm welcome of children to this national landmark.